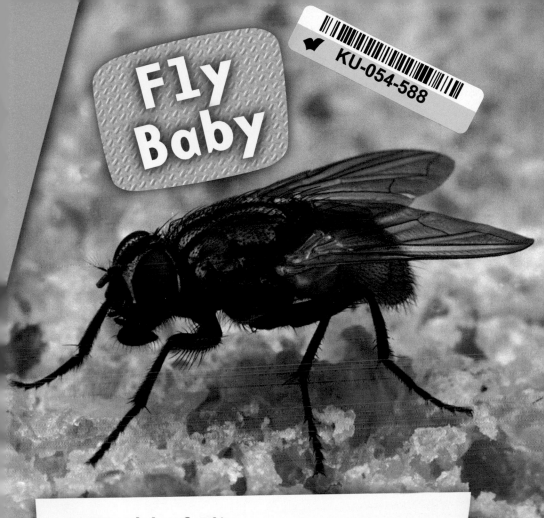

Fly Baby

A World of Flies

The world is full of flies.

There are **thousands** of different kinds of flies in the world.

But where do flies come from?

Maggots

A baby fly comes out of an egg.

It is called a maggot.

It has no wings, no eyes and no legs.

It cannot move far.

It is white and wriggly!

FLY POWER

Contents

Haydn Middleton

Story illustrated by
Fitz Hammond

Heinemann

Find out about

- What flies are like when they are babies
- What flies are like when they are grown-up!

Tricky words

- thousands
- maggot
- wriggly
- breathes
- ceiling
- female

Introduce these tricky words and help the reader when they come across them later!

Text starter

A baby fly is called a maggot. It grows and changes and becomes a fly. Flies carry dirt on their legs which they leave on your food. So watch out for dirty flies!

Maggots love to eat rubbish and poo. That's all they do! They wriggle around and eat yucky things.

Maggot Homes

Maggots live in lots of yucky places. One sort of maggot lives under dirty water. It has a kind of tail, like a straw. It breathes air through this straw.

This maggot will grow into a horsefly.

One sort of maggot lives inside a sheep's nose. It can even eat through to the sheep's eyes and brain!

From Maggots to Flies

Maggots are only white and wriggly for one week.
Then each maggot makes a brown bag around itself.
Inside this bag, the maggot grows and changes.

Then the maggot pops out
of the bag.
It isn't a maggot any more.
It's a young fly!
So what yucky things can a
young fly do?

Flies on the Move

A fly has wings and legs,
so it can fly and walk.
A fly also has sticky feet,
so it can even walk upside down
on the ceiling.

So where does a fly *fly*?
It flies to rubbish and poo.
Then it flies to your house,
and it rubs the rubbish and poo
off its legs and on to your food!

Fly Soup

A fly loves to eat, but it has no teeth.
So it spits all over its food.
This turns the food into yucky soup.
Then the fly walks around in the
soup – and sucks it up!

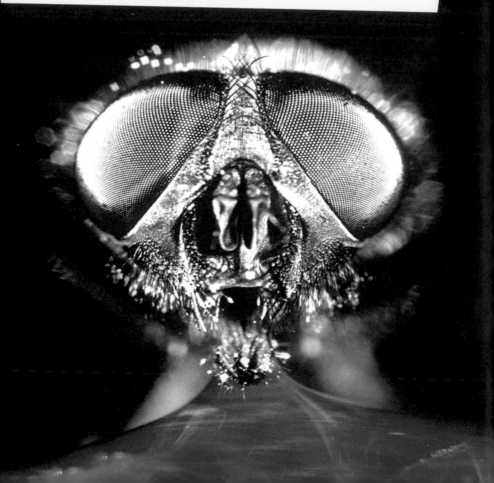

More and More Maggots

A female fly can lay around a hundred eggs at the same time! Out of each egg comes a white maggot.

Each maggot turns into a fly. That is why there are *so **many*** flies in the world!

A lot of flies are called a 'swarm'.

14

Quiz

Text Detective

- What happens to maggots after one week?
- What do you think is the worst thing a fly does?

Word Detective

- **Phonic Focus:** Long vowels
  Page 8: Sound out the three phonemes (sounds) in 'week'. What long vowel can you hear?
- Page 7: Make up a heading for this paragraph.
- Page 12: Why is there a dash between 'soup' and 'and sucks it up'?

Super Speller

Read these words:

more   white   cannot

Now try to spell them!

HA! HA! HA!

 Q Why did the fly fly?

A Because the spider spied her!

Before Reading

In this story

 Sam

 Sam's mum

 A young fly

Tricky words

- kitchen
- shrank
- happened
- suddenly
- aboard
- anywhere

Introduce these tricky words and help the reader when they come across them later!

Story starter

Whenever Sam's mum asks Sam to do a *little* job, he shrinks! One day, Sam's mum asked him to get rid of a fly that was buzzing around.

Shrinking Sam
and the
Fly

Sam was **really** hungry.

"Is dinner ready yet, Mum?" he said.

"Not yet," said Mum.

"I want you to do a little job for me.
A fly is buzzing around in here.
Please shoo it out of the window."
Then Mum went into the kitchen.

Sam knew what would happen next. There was a great big *FLASH* and he shrank!

This always happened when his mum asked him to do a *little* job.

Now Sam was tiny!

But Sam still had to get rid of the fly. Then he would grow to the right size again. But how could he do it?

What do you think Sam will do?

Sam looked up.

The fly was zooming right at him.

It was going to hit him!

Sam shut his eyes and jumped.
Suddenly he landed ... on the fly's
back!

"Welcome aboard!" said the fly.

"Thanks," said Sam, holding on tight.

"It's so cool to zoom around!" said the fly. "When I was a maggot, I couldn't go anywhere. Now I'm a fly and I can zoom **everywhere**!"

"Cool," said Sam.

"Look," said the fly.
"I can go round and round,
up and down, in and out."
Sam began to feel sick.

Suddenly the fly zoomed inside
a lamp. It couldn't get out again!
Round and round and round it
zoomed. Sam felt *really* sick.
How could he get rid of the fly?

"Hey!" cried the fly. "This *isn't* cool. It's hot in here! How do I get out?"

"Fly down!" Sam shouted.

So the fly zoomed down – right out of the light.

"Oh no!" cried the fly. "I'm still hot."
Suddenly, Sam had a great idea.
"You need fresh air!" he shouted.
"Go out of the window!"

"Cool idea!" said the fly, and
it zoomed out of the window.
But it zoomed so fast,
Sam fell off its back ...

... **FLASH!** Sam was the right size again. But he **still** felt sick.

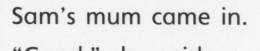

Sam's mum came in.

"Good," she said.

"You did shoo that fly away.

Here's your dinner."

"Sorry," said Sam.
"I don't feel hungry now!"

Quiz

Text Detective

- How did Sam get back to his right size?
- What do you do if you see a fly on your food?

Word Detective

- **Phonic Focus**: Long vowels
  Page 25: Sound out the phonemes (sounds) in 'inside'.
  What long vowel can you hear?
- Page 17: Find a word meaning 'very'.
- Page 22: Why are there dots between 'landed' and
  'on the fly's back!'?

Super Speller

Read these words:

round   gone   threw

Now try to spell them!

HA! HA! HA!

Q How do you get a fly to go away?

 Ask it to buzz off!

32